SHOTOKAN
Advanced Kata

Disclaimer

The publisher of this instructional book WILL NOT BE HELD RESPONSIBLE in any way whatsoever for any physical injury, or damage of any sort, that may occur as a result of reading and/or following the instructions given herein. It is essential therefore, that before attempting any of the physical activities described or depicted in this book, the reader or readers should consult a qualified physician to ascertain whether the reader or readers should engage in the physical activity described or depicted in this book.

As the physical activities described or depicted herein may be overly taxing or sophisticated for the reader or readers, it is *essential that this advice be followed and a physician consulted.*

This high quality educational book is produced by Dragon Books Ltd. London England.

To facilitate learning, high definition photographs have been used throughout, from which distracting background material has been painstakingly removed by expert artists. Printed on fine paper, the book is sewn to allow it to lay flat for easy study without damaging the binding, and is protected against soiling by a laminated cover.

SHOTOKAN
Advanced Kata

Keinosuke Enoeda 8th Dan

Published by
dragon books

Acknowledgements

Photography	Malcolm Copp-Taylor
Layout & Design	Garry O'Keefe B.A. (Hons)
Translation-Introduction	Mrs. Chieko Buck
Equipment	Sakura Trading Company
Author's assistants	I I. Tomita & T. O'Neill

U.S. Distributor Sakura Dragon
Corp., Los Angeles, California

Printed and bound in Great Britain by
Anchor Brendon Ltd, Tiptree, Essex
First published November 1983
Second impression October 1984

Copyright Photography & Design
© Dragon Books Ltd. 1983
Copyright Text
© Keinosuke Enoeda 1983

ISBN 0 946062 04 8
LCCC No. 83-70077

壮鎮 岩鶴 慈院 鉄室小 披塞小

Contents

壮鎮 Sochin	
岩鶴 Gankaku	
慈恩 Jiin	
観空小 Kanku-Sho	
抜塞小 Bassai-Sho	
How to use this book　For your Guidance	
Preface　By M. Nakayama	
Introduction to Kata　Keinosuke Enoeda	

Sochin ... 85
Gankaku ... 65
Jiin ... 49
Kanku-Sho ... 25
Bassai-Sho ... 8
How to use this book ... 6
Preface ... 3
Introduction to Kata ... 1

"Many credited Enoeda with the strongest punch in Japan"

Introduction to Kata

A dictionary definition of Karate Kata might read as follows:—

" A form or exercise in the Japanese martial art of Karate-Do. The performance of a sequence of complex Karate techniques in a precise and regulated manner, in order to meet and repulse the imaginary attacks of multiple assailants. A method of teaching self defence through the use of Karate, a way of exercising and developing the body. "

Such a definition, although precise and informative in the academic sense, does not even hint at the importance or the significance of Kata. In fact, the art of Karate itself was handed down to us from ancient times, largely in the form of Kata, each of which had been refined and perfected over the centuries by the practical experience in combat, and the dedicated practice of long dead Karate masters.

The existence of these elements of personal combat experience, the danger and uncertainty of the times and the consequent need for an effective method of self defence, allowed the Kata to survive in a practical form. Its enforced contact with reality, prevented the Kata degenerating into a meaningless theatrical performance of techniques. Thus it avoided the fate of some schools of Japanese swordsmanship, and other martial arts, that declined into shadows of their former selves during the relatively peaceful centuries of Tokugawa rule. But most important of all, it allowed the Kata to continue to perform their principal function of teaching practical, effective fighting methods.

The legacy of these ancient masters numbers in the region of fifty Kata, each of which reflects not only its time and place of origin, but also the preferences and attitudes of the originator and those who followed in his footsteps through the intervening centuries. Broadly speaking we can divide Kata into two distinct types, those emphasizing fast, light and evasive movements, and those favouring slow, powerful and direct techniques.

The first category teaches the student to control and co-ordinate the movements of his body accurately, and to move fast and effectively with correct timing. The second builds bone, muscle, strength and stamina. It naturally follows therefore, that the regular performance and study of both types of Kata, containing as they do stretching, blocking, kicking and balancing techniques from both categories, will exercise and develop the body in an effective and beneficial way, and at the same time instil genuine fighting ability into the diligent student.

The final point about Kata that I would like to bring to your attention is an important one, that nevertheless is often missed, or not recognised for its importance. It is that etiquette is of the utmost importance in Karate-Do, and must be maintained at all times. Therefore, whenever you practice do so with modesty, but not timidity. Be ready at all times to express yourself through the Kata you are performing by bringing together your mind, body and the movements of the exercise. Avoid however at all costs becoming preoccupied with the rules and method of the performance of the Kata, to the exclusion of the fighting methods that they contain, the learning of which were, and are the principal purpose of these important and exacting exercises.

Notes on the performance of the Kata.

1. Always bow before performing a Kata.
2. Perform the movements in exactly the right sequence, moving in the correct direction at any given time, and starting and finishing on exactly the same spot.
3. Understand precisely the meaning of each movement, and its objective, then attack or defend accordingly. Perform the Kata as authentically as possible by combining the following essential principles:

Correct Adjustment of Power   (hard-soft)
Speed of Technique   (slow-fast)
Flexibility of Body   (tense-relaxed)

Preface by Masatoshi Nakayama Chief Instructor Japan Karate Association.

Preface

It is a matter of great celebration for us all in the Karate world that Mr. Keinosuke Enoeda has published these books on Kata, which represent the fruit of his many years of Karate practice. Mr. Enoeda is one of my fellow founder members of the Japan Karate Association, and I have always found him to be a highly reliable instructor who has represented Karate well wherever he has taught, and striven hard to keep the most distinctive and powerful characteristics of Shotokan Karate-Do alive and flourishing.

Kata is a unique aspect of Oriental Martial Arts. In ancient times an expert or master would fight for his life on the battlefield, and afterwards make good use of the experience gained from fighting. The techniques of Kata thus developed into a system of training which has been passed down to later generations. Kata practice is the main form of training in martial arts in China and Okinawa. Sensei Funakoshi Gichin was the man who first created a system from the martial arts that were practised in Okinawa and developed a Japanese form based on a tripartite training system consisting of: Kihon (basic techniques), Kata (form) and Kumite (sparring).

Kata and Kumite are closely related, in that if you do not practise Kata, your Kumite will suffer. And conversely, if you neglect Kumite, your Kata will be ragged like a scarecrow dancing. In order to practise Kata you must follow Sensei Funakoshi's instructions: it is very important to follow the teaching sequence in the correct order. Success will not come any quicker if you attempt to grapple with the advanced Kata at a single leap, omitting the intervening steps.

First of all, HEIAN Kata should be practised hard until you have understood and mastered the fundamental principles and iron rules for performing the basic Karate techniques, which you have to put to practical use whenever you execute any type of Kata.

TEKKI Kata (literally Iron Knight) teaches you to stand solidly and steadily, first by training the lower part of the body to be strong and solid, and then by using the strength from the waist to reinforce the upper part of the body, thus conveying the power from the hips to the trunk. This Kata may be thought of as a test of endurance.

When you practise HEIAN you develop form and accuracy, and when you practise TEKKI you will develop power and discipline; these qualities will lead you to the more advanced Kata. Next, you should go on to master the seven Kata accurately, methodically and in the right order, just as Sensei Funakoshi adopted them for Shotokan Karate.

You should practise each Kata sufficiently to be able to express and perform freely all of its characteristics. The stability, magnificence and dynamic movement of BASSAI; the ebb and flow of strength in KANKU coupled with the control of speed to produce fast and slow actions, the stretching and contracting of the body and the variation of WAZA or techniques; the dignified and powerful action of JITTE as attacks with a stick are countered; the simultaneous movements of hands and feet, combined with breath control in HANGETSU; the lithe instinctive high and low movements of EMPI; the balancing on one leg of GANKAKU and the action of moving forward and turning, and turning on the spot which must be executed smoothly in JION.

Sensei Funakoshi designated the above fifteen Kata (HEIAN 1.2.3.4.5. TEKKI 1.2.3. BASSAI, KANKU, JITTE, HANGETSU, EMPI, GANKAKU, and JION) as the Shotokan teaching method that would give students every chance of success if they assimilated and mastered it all. You should therefore acquire the basic skills as exactly as possible, without simplifying or modifying them.

Students wishing to learn more must perfect the skills and movements acquired from practising the fifteen Kata, and should then practise each one in accordance with their character or physical constitution, following the instructions in this book. Do this and you will certainly improve, and remember that it is vital to make every effort to keep practising steadily and patiently, without being too eager for results and without being too hasty.

M. Nakayama
Chief Instructor J.K.A.

The author performing a side thrust kick (Yoko-Geri Kekomi) South Africa, 1964.

Lower picture: Master Enoeda performs a side thrust kick counter-attack to South Africa's Stan Schmidt (circa 1964).

Master Enoeda aged 18 in traditional dress.

How to use this book

Please study this section carefully before you read this book.

These notes will help you to get the maximum benefit from this book in the shortest possible time, please follow them from start to finish each time you study.

As with all forms of learning 'little and often' is the most effective way of acquiring knowledge, so commit yourself to ten or fifteen minutes each day, perhaps during your lunch hour, or when you relax after dinner, and you will be surprised and delighted with the progress you make.

1 Read quickly through the Kata that you are studying, look only at the photographs that are marked with a white number on a black circle. These are the fundamental moves of the Kata, and must be committed to memory (Fig.A).

One way to do this is to study each individual photograph carefully, then close your eyes for an instant before moving on to the next, as if the eyes were a camera and the eyelids the shutter.

2 When you are satisfied that you have a basic idea of the sequence of movements, go through the photographs again, this time studying the intermediate photographs as well (see fig.B) so as to understand better the relationship between the fundamental techniques.

5 With the book open in front of you, slowly go through the movements of the Kata, never deviating from the example shown in the text. Perform the whole Kata in your own time to fix the sequence of techniques in your mind.

6 Finally, read the brief introduction that appears at the beginning of the Kata. This will give you some idea of the significance of the Kata, its origin and the specific benefits that will be obtained from its study.

(These figures extracted from Volume 1 of this series.)

67. Perform another right downward block, snapping the left fist up to press against the right upper arm. *Fast.*

68. Look to the right and moving the right foot across to the right, pull both arms back towards your left side...

Side View

3 Go through the whole Kata again including the side view photographs and where appropriate, front view photographs, which, for easy recognition, are divided into fine horizontal lines (Fig.C) and are clearly captioned. These will allow you to study the movements in the Kata that are usually hidden from an observer viewing the performance from the front (ie. facing the performer when he starts the Kata).

4 By now you should have a good idea of the movements of the Kata, so to obtain more detailed information read the numbered captions related to each movement which contain information not apparent from the photograph. There is guidance on timing for example, or the sequence in which the movement must be performed.

7 Carry what you have learnt from the text into class study. It will help you to make rapid progress, and prevent you from copying the bad habits of your less knowledgeable classmates which if acquired, are so difficult to rid oneself of.

8 From time to time, go back to your book and check that you are still performing the Kata correctly. This occasional reference to the text will prevent you from deviating from perfect technique.

Bassai Sho

'To storm a castle and capture the enemy'

By the powerful, energetic and determined execution of this Kata, the performer demonstrates his total physical and spiritual commitment to storming the castle of his enemy, and capturing him. The impression created by the performance of the Kata must be one of such dynamic power, spiritual strength and unshakable resolve, that the fall of the castle becomes inevitable, and further resistance useless. Bassai Sho contains many offensive and defensive techniques, and is especially effective in teaching defence against a staff or similar weapon.

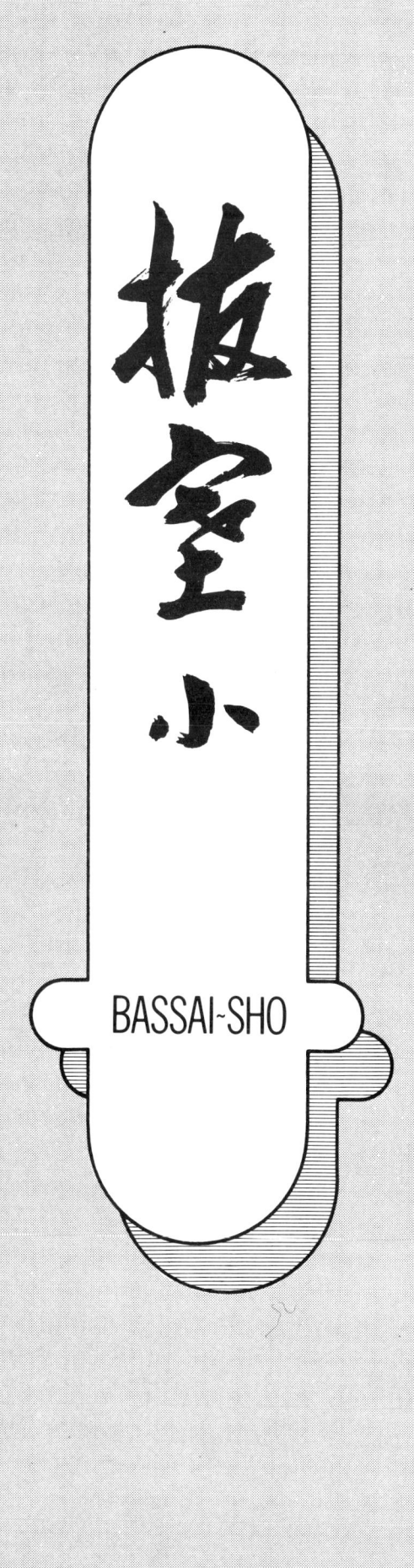

BASSAI-SHO

Bassai-Sho

1. Natural stance.

2. (YOI) Move the right foot to the left and place the left open hand edge (palm facing right) on top of the thumb of the right open hand (palm facing left). *Slow.*

3. Swing both arms back to the left side twisting the left hand at the wrist to rest on the right, and lift the right foot...

6. ...land in a right back stance and position both arms as shown – both hands with palms turned upward. *Fast.*

Side View

7. Pull the right arm down and across to the right side twisting the wrist, at the same time raise the left arm upward on the same vertical line until both arms are on the same level. *Slow.*

Bassai-Sho

4. ... step forward into a crossed stance and with the right hand high above head level as shown, perform a double block left palm pressed against the right wrist. *Fast*.

Side View

5. Look 180° to the left and move the left foot in that direction, moving both hands over to the left side...

Side View

8. Turn 270° around to the right, moving the right foot back to the left foot and swinging the right arm – hand open...

9. ... in a big anti-clockwise circle with the palm facing up throughout – dip the knees at the same time...

Bassai-Sho

10. ... continue the swing upward over the head as the body straightens and close the hand into a fist ...

11. ... swing the right arm across the body – anti-clockwise and perform a downward block to the right side. *Fast*.

12. Step forward with the left foot opening both hands and ...

16. ... left side, perform a sweeping block with the knife-hand as the feet come together the back of the right open hand rests on top of the left fist. *Fast*.

17. Perform a simultaneous side snap kick and ridge hand strike. *Fast*.

18. Step down into a straddle-leg stance facing the front and cross the left open hand under the right arm ...

Bassai-Sho

13. ... landing in a right back stance position both arms as shown – both hands with palms turned upward. *Fast*.

14. Pull the right arm down and across to the right side – twisting the wrist, at the same time raise the left arm until both arms are on the same level. *Slow*.

15. Pull the left foot back to the right and swing the right open hand out and round to the ...

19. ... sweep the left hand in front of the body performing a vertical knife hand block. *Slow*.

20. Perform a right middle-area punch ...

21. ... and a left middle-area punch in a double action. *Fast*.

Bassai-Sho

22. Turn 90° to the left switching your weight back on to your right leg, pivoting the left foot around and cross left arm over the right...

23. ...land in a right back stance and perform a double block, left downward block and right inside block to head level. *Fast*.

24. Turn 180° to the right, switching your weight back on to your left leg whilst pivoting both feet and cross right arm over your left...

28. Step forward with the left foot, crossing the left arm over right...

29. ...land in a right back stance and perform a left knife-hand block. *Fast*.

30. Step forward with the right foot, crossing the right arm over the left...

25. ...land in a left back stance and perform a double block-right downward block and left inside block to head level. *Fast*.

26. Look 90° to the left (to face front), move the left foot halfway toward the right and cross the right arm over the left (hands open)...

27. ...land in a left back stance and perform a knife-hand block. *Fast*.

31. ...land in a left back stance and perform a right knife-hand block. *Fast*.

32. Step back with the right foot, crossing the left arm over the right...

33. ...land in a right back stance and perform a left knife-hand block. *Fast*.

Bassai-Sho

34. Move the left foot across to the left, switching your weight forward as you do so and swing your right arm under the left...

35. ...in a circular motion and as the right arm goes high, the left hand catches the right wrist (fingers and thumb on top) and pulls downwards...

36. ...land in a left front stance and perform a grasping block. *Slow. Note: The hips are twisted to the left.*

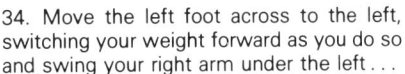

40. ...step back and downward into a right back stance and twisting both wrists outward, perform a reverse wedge block. *Fast.*

Side View

41. Slide both feet forward and perform a double punch to face level. *Fast.*

37. Lift the right knee up between the arms...

38. ... and pulling both fists back to the right side of the chest (palms up) perform a side thrust kick to the lower level. *Fast*.

39. Pull your foot back and turn to the rear (180° to the left), crossing the arms in front of the body...

Side View

42. Snap both fists back to the same position – all one action. *Fast*.

Side View

Bassai-Sho

43. Swing the right leg up and around and perform a crescent kick, at the same time pull both arms back as shown – the right arm performing a swinging outside block. *Fast*.

Side View

44. Land in a straddle-leg stance and pull both fists to the left side – the right vertical fist on top of the left fist...

46. Look to the front (180° to the left) and cross the left arm under the right...

47. ... perform a left hammer-fist. *Fast*.

48. Step forward with the right foot...

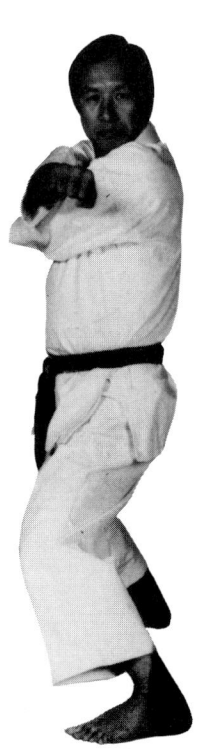

Bassai-Sho

Side View

45. ... thrust both fists to the right side in a double punch. *Fast.*

Side View

49. ... land in a right front stance performing a stepping punch *(Oi-tsuki). Fast.*

50. Look to the rear (180° to the left) and shifting your weight onto the left leg ...

51. ... swing the right leg and right arm up and around performing a simultaneous crescent kick and swinging outside block. *Fast.*

Bassai-Sho

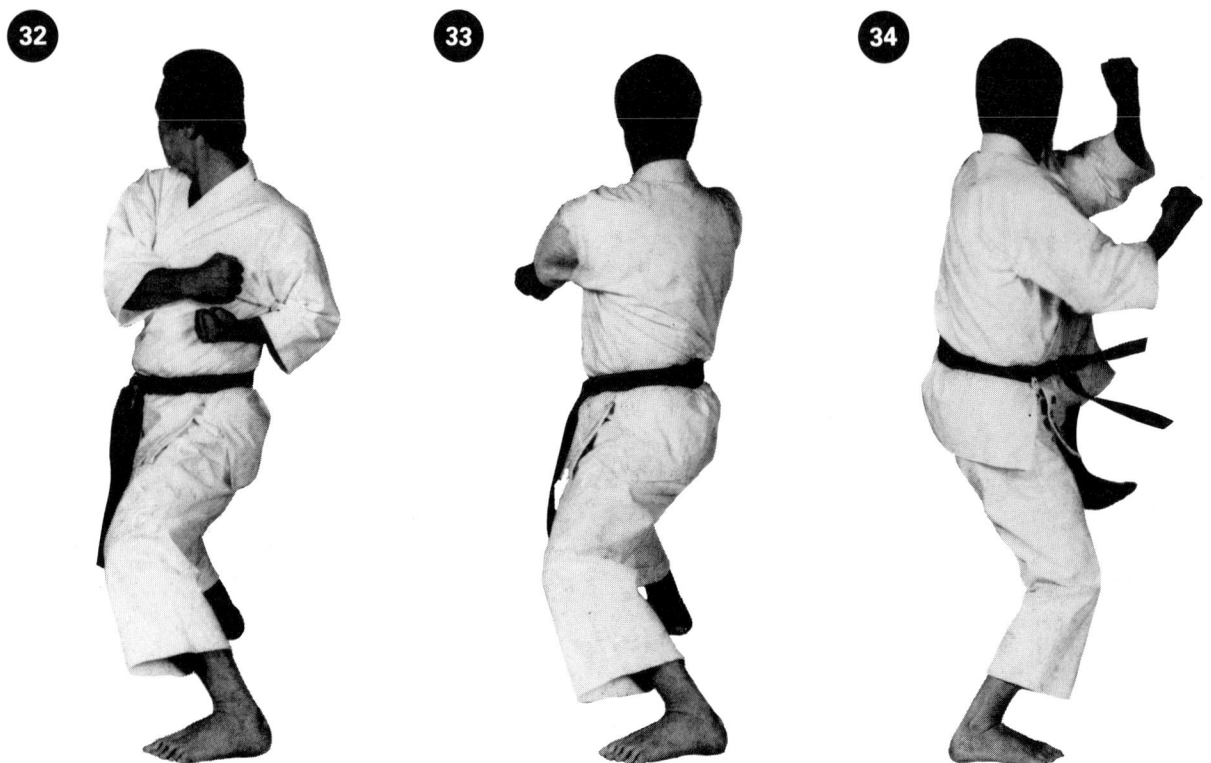

52. Land in a straddle-leg stance and pull both fists to the left side...

53. ...thrust both fists out to the right side in a double punch. *Fast.*

54. Swing the left leg and left arm up and around — perform a simultaneous crescent kick and swinging outside block. *Fast.*

56. ...thrust both fists out to the left side in a double punch. *Fast.*

Side View

57. Swinging the right leg and arm up and around, perform a crescent kick and swinging outside block.

Bassai-Sho

Side View

55. Land in a straddle-leg stance and pull both fists to the right side – the left vertical fist on top of the right fist...

Side View

58. Land in a straddle leg stance and pull both fists to the left side...

59. ...thrust both fists out to the right side in a double punch. *Fast.*

60. Turn to face 225° around to the left and drawing the left foot in toward the right leg slightly, open the right hand and cross the left arm under it...

Bassai-Sho

61. Push the left foot out and around in a small circular motion, sweep the left arm (hand open) higher than the right arm...

62. ... pull the foot back into a cat stance and pull both arms downward to the position shown – both hands turned so that the palms face inward. *Slow*.

63. Look 90° to the right and move the left foot across in that direction, the left open hand in front of you, the right across the body under the left arm.

67. Move the right foot out into the natural stance, finishing position (YAME).

Please Note

The numbers shown in brackets refer to the similarly numbered captions in the main Kata section. After studying each application turn back to the relevant movement to understand how it fits into the overall exercise.

64. Push the right foot out and around in a circular motion, sweep the right arm higher than the left arm . . .

65. . . . pull the foot back into a cat stance and pull both arms downward to the position shown. *Slow*.

66. Look to the front, and move the right foot back to the left foot. Place the edge of the left open hand on top of the thumb edge of the right open hand.

Applications

1. (4) As the attack is made, assume a crossed stance and with the left palm pressed against the right wrist in a double block, move your weight forward to counter the blow, and deflect the attack.

2. (6) Adopt a right back stance as your opponent attacks with a staff, and with palms upwards, catch the weapon with the left hand extended forwards, and right held above the head.

Bassai-Sho — Applications

3. From Application 2. With premise timing, pull the right arm down, twisting the wrist, and the left arm up to break your opponent's balance and throw him forward.

4. (17) A simultaneous ridge hand strike to his wrist, and kick to his face counters your opponent's left punch attack.

5. (43) As your opponent steps in with a right punch, stop his attack with a swinging block, at the same time sweeping his right foot before it touches the floor.

6. From Application 5. As your opponent launches a reverse punch attack, thrust your arms out to the side, the right to block the punch, and the left to attack your antagonist.

KANKU-SHO

Kanku Sho

As with the similar Kanku Dai, this Kata contains many varied techniques and movements, the most characteristic of which are the smoothly changing turns. From the performance of this Kata, aim to acquire the skills of stretching and contracting the body, control of speed to produce fast and slow techniques, production and dissipation of power, and the ability to jump, land, spring up and turn. Kanku Sho can be clearly differentiated from the related Kanku Dai Kata by the amount of 'chudan' (chest area techniques) it contains, compared to the 'jodan' (upper level) techniques of the latter.

Kanku-Sho

1. Natural stance.
2. Cross your arms in front of the body...
3. ... to the starting position. (YOI).

4. Look to the left and step to the right with the right foot, swinging both arms to the right side...
5. ... land in a right back stance and perform a left inside block, the right fist supporting the inside of the left elbow. *Fast*.
6. Look over the right shoulder and swing both arms to the left side...

Kanku-Sho

7. ... slide both feet to the left and perform a right inside block, the left fist supporting the right elbow.

8. Look to the front and moving the right leg back and around to the right, swing both arms to the right side ...

9. ... slide both feet back into a right back stance and perform a left inside block, right fist supporting the left elbow. *Fast.*

13. ... to perform an inside block. *Fast.*

14. Step forward with the left foot ...

15. ... into a left front stance and perform a left punch to the middle. *Fast.*

Kanku-Sho

10. Step forward with the right foot...

11. ...into a right front stance and perform a right punch to the middle. *Fast*.

12. Without moving the left arm, instantly bend the right elbow and snap the right fist inside then outwards...

16. Without moving the right arm, instantly bend the left elbow and snap the left fist inward then outwards...

17. ...to perform an inside block. *Fast*.

18. Step forward with the right foot...

Kanku-Sho

19. ... into a right stepping punch to the middle. *Fast*.

20. Turn 180° to the left (to face the opposite direction) and move the left foot across to the left – at the same time swinging the right arm in an upward arc ...

21. ... as the right arm goes high catch the wrist with your left hand (fingers and thumb on top) and twist the right open hand to the right as you pull downwards with both arms ...

Side View

24. Step forward and down, bringing the left foot (heel raised) up behind the right foot into a crossed stance and strike to the front with the right back fist. *Fast*.

Side View

Kanku-Sho

22. ... to the position shown, in front of your chest, perform a grasping block. *Slow.* Note: The hips are twisted to the left.

Side View

23. Perform a right front snap kick whilst simultaneously pulling the hands (closing them into fists) back to the right side – left vertical fist on top of the right fist. *Fast.*

25. Step backwards with the left foot and cross the right arm under the left ...

Side View

26. ... land in a right front stance and perform an inside block. *Fast.*

Kanku-Sho

Side View   27. Perform a left reverse punch. *Fast*...   Side View

30. ... land in a right back stance and perform a simultaneous left downward block and right inside block to the right side. *Fast*.

31. Cross the left arm over the right arm...

32. ... slowly pull the left foot back toward the right foot, raising the body whilst performing a left downward block – pulling the right fist back to the side. *Slow*.

28. ... and a right front punch. *Fast.*

Side View

29. Turn 180° to the left to face the opposite direction and move the left foot into a right back stance crossing the left arm above the right...

33. Step to the left with the left foot and forward into a left front stance, while swinging the right arm (hand open) in an upward arc across the body...

34. ... as the right arm goes high, catch the wrist with your left hand...

35. ... and twist the right open hand to the right as you pull downwards with both hands...

Kanku-Sho

36. ... perform a grasping block. *Slow.*

37. Perform a right front snap-kick whilst simultaneously pulling the hands (closing them into fists) back to the right side – as before – *Fast.*

38. Step forward lowering the body, and perform a back fist strike to the front with the right hand.

42. ... and a right front punch. *Fast.*

43. Turn 180° to the left (to face the opposite direction) and move the left foot into a right back stance crossing the left arm over the right ...

Side View

Kanku-Sho

39. Move the left foot backwards and cross the right arm under the left arm...

40. ...land in a right front stance and perform an inside block. *Fast.*

41. Perform a left reverse punch. *Fast...*

44. ...land in a right back stance and perform a simultaneous left downward block and right inside block to the right side. *Fast.*

Side View

45. Cross the left arm over the right arm...

Kanku-Sho

Side View

46. ... slowly pull the left foot back toward the right foot, raising the body whilst performing a left downward block pulling the right fist back to the side. *Slow*.

Side View

Front View

50. ... in a continuous action, slide both feet to the left, shifting the weight and changing the stance to a straddle-leg stance, thrust both fists to the left side. *Fast*.

Front View

47. Turn 90° to the left and move the left foot across to the left into a right back stance crossing the left arm over the right arm...

48. ...perform a simultaneous left downward block and right high inside block which finishes behind the head. *Fast*.

49. Pull both fists back to the right side in a reaction and...

51. Turn your head 180° to the right (to face the opposite direction) and cross the right arm over the left arm...

52. ...shift more weight back to the left leg, changing to a left back stance and perform a simultaneous right downward block and left high inside block which finishes behind the head. *Fast*.

53. Pull both fists back to the left side in a reaction and...

Kanku-Sho

Front View

54. ... in a continuous action, slide both feet to the right, shifting the weight and changing to a straddle-leg stance, thrust both fists to the right side. *Fast*.

Front View

57. Sliding both feet forward still maintaining a left back stance, twist both arms in an anti-clockwise direction...

Side View

58. ... and thrusting the right arm forward, pull the left hand into the body as shown. *Fast*. Note: both hands are closed into half fists.

55. Looking 90° to the left, move the left foot half way to the right, and moving the right foot across to the left, open both hands and swing both arms to the front of the body...

Side View

56. ...land in a left back stance with the left hand (palm open) in front of the forehead and the right hand (palm facing up and thumb extended) above the right knee as shown. *Slow.*

59. Leap up and back around to the left in an anti-clockwise direction...

Side View

60. ...crossing the right arm (palm open to the left ear) over the left arm...

Kanku-Sho

61. ... land in a left back stance (in a position behind the previous stance) and perform a right knife-hand block. *Fast*.

Side View

62. Look to the left and pull both arms to the right side – left vertical fist on the right fist – whilst drawing the left foot up to the right knee...

66. ... continue the action by performing a simultaneous right side snap kick and back fist strike. *Fast*.

67. As you land in a right front stance, perform a left elbow strike into the right open palm. *Fast*.

68. Turn 90° to the left, pivoting on both feet and circling the right arm (hand open) under the left arm in an upward arc in front of the body...

Kanku-Sho

63. ... continue the action by performing a simultaneous left side snap kick and back fist strike. *Fast*.

64. As you land in a left front stance perform a right elbow strike into the left open palm. *Fast*.

65. Look to the right and pull both arms to the left side – right vertical fist on the left fist – whilst drawing the right foot up to the left knee ...

69. ... as the right arm goes high, catch the wrist with your left hand ...

70. ... and twist the right open hand to the right as you pull downwards with both hands and perform a grasping block. *Slow*.

71. Perform a right front snap kick whilst simultaneously pulling the hands (closed into fists) back to the right side. *Fast*.

Kanku-Sho

72. Step forward and down into a crossed stance and snap the right back fist to the front. *Fast.*

Side View

73. Move the left foot backwards and cross the right arm under the left arm . . .

78. . . . lean your body over the right knee whilst pulling the right fist back to the side and slowly swinging the left arm (hand open) out and upward away from the body.. *Slow.*

74. . . . land in a right front stance and perform a right inside block. *Fast.*

Side View

Kanku-Sho

75. Perform a left reverse punch. *Fast*...

76. ... and a right front punch. *Fast*.

77. Look behind you and without moving the legs, cross the left arm (hand open) under the right arm... *Slow*.

79. ... leap up and around to the left in an anti-clockwise direction, performing a crescent jump kick in mid air with the right foot into the left palm...

80. Land in the deep position shown – right knee deeply bent – left leg extended straight back and both arms to the front – palms flat – look to the front. *Fast*.

Side View

Kanku-Sho

81. Quickly reverse the feet – your body stays in the same place – and cross the left arm over the right arm – both hands open...

Side View

82. ... land in a deep right back stance and swing both arms to the left side – the left arm straight with palm facing down and the right arm with palm facing up. *Fast.*

Side View

85. Turn 270° around to the left, pivoting on the right foot and moving the left foot in and around to the left, whilst crossing the left arm under the right arm...

86. ... land in a left front stance and perform a left inside block. *Fast.*

Kanku-Sho

Side View

83. Move the right foot forward crossing the right arm (open hand) over the left arm...

84. ...land in a left back stance and perform a right knife-hand block. *Fast*.

87. Move the right foot forward...

88. ...land in a right front stance and perform a right stepping punch. *Fast*.

89. Look 180° to the right (to face the opposite direction) pivoting on the left foot, move the right foot around to the right, crossing the right arm under the left arm...

Kanku-Sho

90. ... land in a right front stance and perform a right inside block. *Fast*.

91. Step forward with the left foot ...

92. ... land in a left front stance and perform a left stepping punch. *Fast*.

93. Look to the front and crossing the arms in front of your body, pull the left foot back ...

94. ... to the starting position. (YAME).

Applications Kanku-Sho

1. (23) Having blocked the attacker's punch, use your right hand augmented by your left, to catch his hand and pulling it down to your right, kick him strongly in the face.

2. (30) Counter the attack by adopting a back stance and performing a downward block with the left arm, which is balanced and strengthened by the simultaneous performance of an inside block with the right.

3. (56) As the frontal attack is made with the staff, assume a left back stance and catch the weapon with both hands as shown, palms upwards.

4. (58) From Application 3. Having seized the weapon, twist your arms anti-clockwise to force your opponent back, and break his balance.

Kanku-Sho — Applications

5. (79) After successfully blocking your opponent's right handed attack with the back of your left hand, jump high and perform a crescent kick to strike him with the sole of your foot.

6. (79,80) From Application 5. As you land on your hands and right foot attack with a powerful back thrust kick.

JIIN

Jiin

As with the similar Jion Kata, this exercise takes its name from the Jion Temple in ancient China (Jion-Ji) where, it is believed, the oriental martial arts as we know them, were born. Much practice is necessary if the forward movements and turns, which must be performed smoothly and gently, but with great strength and spirit, are to be mastered. The timing of the turning movements must also be studied closely.

Jin

1. Natural Stance.

2. Move the feet together and wrap the left hand around the right fist – elbows bent and fist at jaw level – to make the ready position (YOI).

3. Cross the arms, right over left...

4. ...step back with the left foot to land in a right front stance and perform a simultaneous left arm inside block and a right arm downward sweeping block. *Fast.*

5. Look 90° to the left and step to the left, crossing the left arm over the right arm...

6. ...land in a right back stance and perform a simultaneous left downward block and a right high inside block which finishes behind your head. *Fast.*

Jiin

7. Look 180° around to the right and pivoting to the right, cross the right arm over the left arm...

8. ...shifting the weight onto the left leg, land in a left back stance and perform a simultaneous right downward block and left high inside block. *Fast.*

9. Look 135° around to the left and pulling the left fist back to the side, extend the right hand upward...

13. Look 90° to the right and moving the right foot in that direction, pull the right foot back to the side and extend the left hand upward...

14. ...land in a right front stance and perform a right rising block. *Fast.*

15. Move the left foot forward...

10. ... shifting the weight onto the left leg move into a left front stance and perform a left rising block. *Fast*.

11. Step forward with the right foot...

12. ... land in a right front stance and perform a right stepping punch. *Fast*.

16. ... land in a left front stance and perform a left stepping punch. *Fast*.

17. Look 45° to the left and moving the left foot in that direction, cross the left arm over the right arm...

18. ... land in a left front stance and perform a left downward block. *Fast*.

Jiin

19. Step forward with the right foot, swinging the right open hand out to the side...

20. ...pivoting the hips, land in a straddle-leg stance, and perform a right knife-hand strike to the middle level. *Fast*.

21. Move the left foot forward whilst swinging the left open hand (palm turned away) out to the side...

Side View

25. Look 225° around to the left and moving the left foot across to the left, cross both arms (palms facing inwards)...

26. ...land in a left front stance and perform a wedge block with both arms. *Slow*.

Jiin

 KIAI

22. ... pivoting the hips, land in a straddle leg stance and perform a left knife-hand strike. *Fast.*

23. Move the right foot forward whilst swinging the right open hand (palm turned away) to the side ...

24. ... pivoting the hips, land in a straddle-leg stance, and perform a right knife-hand strike. *Fast.*

27. Without moving the arms perform a right front kick to the middle area. *Fast.*

28. As the foot snaps back, step forward ...

29. ... land in a right front stance and perform a right stepping punch. *Fast* ...

Jiin

30. ... and a left reverse punch. *Fast*.

31. Without moving the legs, cross the right arm over the left...

32. ... and perform a simultaneous right downward block and a left inside block. *Fast*.

36. ... as the foot snaps back step forward...

37. ... land in a left front stance and perform a left stepping punch. *Fast*...

38. ... and a right reverse punch. *Fast*.

33. Look 90° to the right and moving the right foot in that direction, cross both arms (palms facing inward)...

34. ... land in a right front stance and perform a wedge block with both arms. *Slow.*

35. Without moving the arms, perform a left front kick to the middle area. *Fast*...

39. Without moving the legs cross the left arm over the right arm...

40. ... and perform a simultaneous left downward block and a right inside block. *Fast.*

41. Turn 315° around to the right, pivoting on the left foot and moving the right foot around in that direction whilst crossing the right arm under the left...

Jiin

42. ... land in a straddle leg stance and perform a right hammer-fist strike to the middle area. *Fast*.

43. Turn 360° around to the left, pivoting on the right foot and moving the left foot around in that direction whilst crossing the left arm under the right arm ...

44. ... land in a straddle-leg stance and perform a left hammer-fist strike. *Fast*.

47. Look 45° to the left and move the left foot in that direction whilst crossing the left arm (hand open) under the right arm ...

48. ... land in a left diagonal straddle-leg stance (SOCHIN STANCE) and perform a left vertical knife-hand block. *Slow*.

49. Shifting more weight onto the front leg, land in a left front stance and perform a right reverse punch. *Fast* ...

45. Move the right foot forward and without moving the head cross the right arm under the left arm . . .

46. . . . land in a straddle-leg stance and perform a right hammer-fist strike. *Fast*.

Side View

50. . . . and a left straight punch. *Fast*.

51. Perform a right front kick to the middle area . . .

52. . . . snap the foot back . . .

Jiin

53. ... and step back into the same place, performing a right reverse punch as you land. *Fast*.

54. Cross the left arm over the right arm ...

55. ... and perform a simultaneous left downward block and a right inside block. *Fast*.

59. Without moving the right arm cross the left fist to the right ear ...

60. ... perform a left arm downward block. *Fast*.

61. Cross both arms in front of the chest, left arm over the right arm ...

56. Look 135° to the left and pivoting on the right foot, move the left foot around in that direction whilst crossing the left arm under the right arm...

57. ...continue stepping around until the left foot is in line with the right...

58. ...land in a straddle-leg stance and perform a simultaneous right downward block and a left inside block. *Fast*.

62. ...and perform a double inside block with both arms. *Slow*.

63. Perform a left straight punch to the face. *Fast*.

64. ...and a right straight punch to the middle. *Fast*.

65. Move the left foot to the right and wrap the left hand around the right fist, to assume the finishing position. (YAME).

66. Assume the natural stance.

Applications

Jiin

1. (4) As the attack is made, assume a forward stance by stepping backwards with the left foot, then block the kick with a right down block, balanced and strengthened by the simultaneous performance of an inside block with the left arm.

2. (26) Prevent your opponent seizing you at chest level by uncrossing your arms (25) and performing a block by twisting them both outwards.

3. (27) From Application 2. Having prevented him seizing you, counter-attack immediately with a kick to his stomach.

4. (42) As your opponent attacks from an angle of about 45°, turn into him, grabbing the attacking hand, and simultaneously striking his body with your right.

Gankaku

'A crane standing on a rock'

The two characters with which this name is written, are the Chinese ideograms for a rock, and the bird known as the crane. Combined, they allude to the crane, standing in its characteristic, one legged stance from which comes the name Gankaku. Imagine this beautiful and seemingly harmless bird, on a high crag, and standing on one leg, confronting his enemy and preventing his attack by projecting an aura of immense superiority. Imagine also as he concentrates all his power into his legs, wings and beak, in preparation for his own attack. Consider what a fierce adversary even a beautiful and harmless bird can be when confronted by an enemy. This is what the originator of this unique Kata wanted us to feel when we perform Gankaku.

GANKAKU

Gankaku

1. Natural stance.

2. Cross the arms in front of the body...

3. ... to the starting position (YOI).

7. ... with the left hand on top, press both hands downward in a continuous movement...

8. ... and perform a left straight punch — pulling the right fist back to the hip. *Fast.*

9. Perform a right reverse punch to the middle area. *Fast.*

Gankaku

4. Step back with the right foot and move both open hands to the right...

5. ...land in a right back stance and perform a side combined block to the left side at face level. The backs of the hands are pressed together with the right palm on the outside. *Fast.*

6. Rotate the right hand in and around the left hand, until the palms are facing...

10. Swing the right foot forward and around to the right, pivoting on the left foot...

11. ...turn 180° around to the left and simultaneously raise the right foot and the right arm.

12. Perform a stamping kick as you land in a straddle-leg stance and a simultaneous right downward sweeping block. *Fast.*

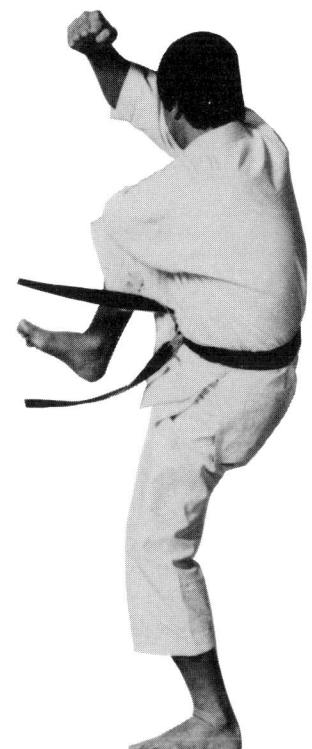

Gankaku

Side View

13. Turn 180° around to the left and step to the left with the left foot...

14. ... land in a left front stance and perform a high cross block hands open. *Fast*.

18. ... perform a left jumping front kick. *Fast*...

19. ... both feet landing on the floor and both arms – with the wrists still pressed together – are pulled back to the right side...

20. ... and upon landing in a left front stance, perform a low cross block to the front. *Fast*.

Gankaku

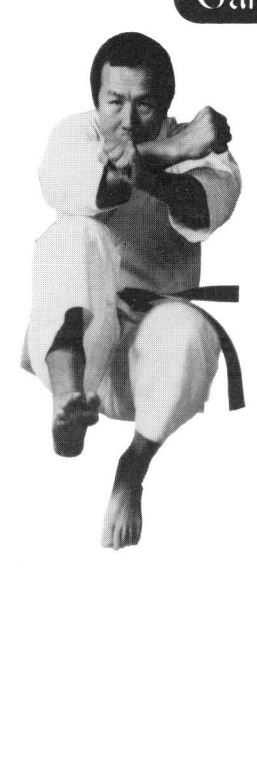

15. Pull the arms down to chest height closing the hands into fists. *Slow*.

16. Leap into the air and perform a right jumping front kick...

17. ... as the right foot snaps back...

21. Turn 180° around to the right and step the left foot around to the right whilst simultaneously pulling the crossed arms back to the right side...

22. ... continue stepping the left foot forward...

23. ... land in a left front stance and perform another low cross block. *Fast*.

Gankaku

Side View

24. Turn 180° to the right and stepping the right foot to the right, cross the right arm over the left arm . . .

25. . . . land in a left back stance and perform a right downward block – the left arm makes the same motion and finishes across the body as shown, the back of the fist pointing downwards. *Fast.*

29. . . . land in a right front stance and perform a wedge block with both arms. *Slow.*

30. Look 90° to the left and step the left foot back in line with the right foot, crossing the arms – hands open – in front of the body . . .

31. . . . land in a straddle-leg stance and perform a reverse wedge block with both arms, hands open, palms up. *Slow.*

Gankaku

26. Step the left foot forward crossing the left arm over the right and opening both hands...

27. ... land in a right back stance, and perform a left open hand downward block – the right open hand makes the same motion and finishes as shown. *Fast*.

28. Step the right foot forward crossing the arms – hands still open – in front of the body...

Front View

32. Slightly move the left foot in towards the right and whilst raising the body up, cross the arms above the head...

33. ... look 90° over the left shoulder and lower both arms out to the sides. *Slow*.

Gankaku

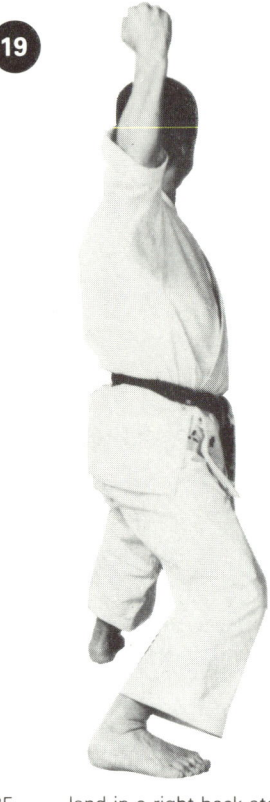

Side View | 34. Step to the left with the left foot whilst crossing the left arm over the right arm... | 35. ...land in a right back stance and perform a simultaneous left downward block and right high inside block, which finishes behind the head. *Fast*.

Side View | 38. Turn 360° around to the left, step back and around with the left foot, whilst crossing the left arm over the right arm... | 39. ...land in a right back stance and perform a simultaneous left downward block and a right high inside block. *Fast*.

Gankaku

Side View

36. Step forward with the right foot and cross the right arm over the left arm...

37. ...land in a left back stance and perform a simultaneous right downward block and a left high inside block. *Fast*.

Side View

40. Look 90° to the right and move the right foot behind the left, pulling both fists back to the side...

41. ...dropping the body down as shown, perform a low cross block. *Fast*.

Gankaku

42. Step to the right with the right foot, crossing the arms in front of the body . . .

43. . . . land in a straddle-leg stance and perform a reverse wedge block with both arms. *Slow.*

Front View

46. Place both fists — knuckles inward — on the hips, pointing the elbows out to the sides.

Front View

47. Pivot the feet and body to the left (like a left front stance) without moving the head and perform a right elbow block. *Fast* . . .

Gankaku

44. Slightly move the right foot in toward the left and raising the body up, cross the arms above your head...

45. ...lower both arms out to the sides. *Slow.*

Front View

Front View

48. ...then pivot the feet and body to the right and perform a left elbow block. *Fast.*

Front View

Gankaku

49. Turn 180° to the right and move the left foot in behind the right, whilst crossing the arms in front of the body . . .

50. . . . land in a crossed stance and perform a reverse wedge block with both arms.

Front View

54. . . . to rest on top of the right fist which is pulled back to the side. *Slow.*

55. Perform a simultaneous left side snap kick and a left back fist strike to the side . . . *Fast.*

56. . . . return the left foot to the right knee . . .

Gankaku

51. Look 90° to the left and cross the left arm over the right arm...

52. ...lift the left foot up until it rests on and behind the right knee and as the body rises up perform a simultaneous left downward block and a right high inside block. *Slow.*

53. In a big motion bring the left arm over and down...

57. ...move the left foot down, keeping the left arm extended...

58. ...step forward with the right foot into a right front stance and perform a right stepping punch. *Fast.*

59. Draw the right foot back and cross the right arm over the left arm...

32 KIAI

Gankaku

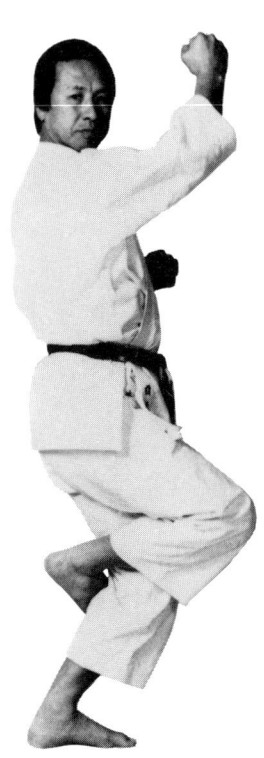

60. ... place the right foot behind the left knee and perform a simultaneous right downward block and a left high inside block. *Slow*.

61. In a big motion bring the right arm over and down ...

62. ... to rest on top of the left fist, which is pulled back to the side. *Slow*.

66. Look 180° to the left and move the left foot back to the right, crossing the left arm over the right arm ...

67. ... place the left foot behind the right knee and perform a simultaneous left downward block and a right high inside block. *Slow*.

Side View

Gankaku

63. Perform a simultaneous side snap kick and a right back fist strike. *Fast* . . .

64. . . . return the right foot to the left knee . . .

65. . . . step down into a straddle-leg stance and pulling the right fist back to the side perform a left reverse punch. *Fast.*

68. In a big motion bring the left arm over and down . . .

69. . . . to rest on top of the right fist which is pulled back to the side. *Slow.*

Side View

Gankaku

70. Perform a simultaneous left side snap kick and a left back fist strike. *Fast*...

71. ...return the left foot to the right knee...

72. ...step down into a straddle-leg stance and perform a right reverse punch. *Fast*.

75. Perform a left rising elbow strike into the palm of the right hand. *Fast*.

76. Pull both hands back to the left hip – the left hand is open and the right fist is pressed into it. *Fast*.

Side View

Gankaku

Side View

73. Look 180° to the right, and step to the right with the right foot...

74. ...land in a right front stance and perform a right knife-hand strike or block to the upper level. *Fast*.

77. Perform a high cross block — hands open — begin to turn the body to the right...

78. ...turn 180° around to the right, pivoting on the right foot, bring the left foot forward and around to the right and place the left foot behind the right knee...

79. ...bring the arms down as shown with the left fist resting on top of the right fist...

Gankaku

80. ... perform a simultaneous left side snap kick and a left back fist strike. *Fast*.

81. Return the left foot to the right knee ...

82. ... put the left foot down, keeping the left arm extended ...

85. ... cross both arms over the head and ...

86. ... return to Natural Stance, the finishing position. (YAME).

Gankaku

KIAI

Side View

83. ... step forward with the right foot into a right front stance and perform a right stepping punch. *Fast.*

84. Turn 180° around to the left and moving the left foot around to the left ...

Applications

1. (5) Step back with your right foot into a back stance and perform a combined block to the side with the backs of your hands pressed together, the right palm facing outwards, to deflect your attacker's left punch.

2. From Application 1. Circle your right hand around your left, and with palms touching, left hand on top, press down to execute the block.

3. (8) From Application 2. Against your opponent's right reverse punch, perform a left punch to deflect the attack and counter-attack at the same time.

Sokumen-Awase-uke

Gankaku — Applications

4. (9) From Application 3. Follow up with a reverse punch to the stomach.

5. (29) As your opponent attempts to seize you at chest level, cross your arms at the wrists with hands open, and push outwards and to the sides so that your palms are eventually facing forward, to prevent him taking hold.

6. (41) As the mid-level front kick comes in, drop down low, and block it with a cross block.

7. (48) As the right front punch is launched, pivot the feet and body to the right, and without moving the head, block the blow with a left elbow block.

8. (63) Block your antagonist's left front punch with your right back fist strike, at the same instant attacking his face with a right snap kick.

9. (77, 79) Countering your opponent's punch with a right knife hand block, attack with a left rising elbow strike to his chin. Pulling his right wrist down to your left, push his arm upward and turn to the right, pivoting on your right foot to bring his arm over your head and onto your right shoulder.

SOCHIN

Sochin

This Kata takes its name from the 'Sochin Dachi' stance that is its most prominent feature. Involving much subtle tightening of the muscles, which must be performed in a calm and gradual fashion, movement when made must alternate between the tense and the explosive. The resultant combination of these factors gives this Kata great depth and feeling. When performing Sochin, it is imperative that **you do not** raise or arch the soles of the feet, but grip the floor as firmly as possible, with the knees pushed strongly in the same direction as your toes.

Sochin

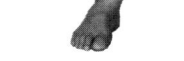

1. Natural Stance.

2. Cross arms in front of body...

3. ...to the starting position (YOI).

4. Raise the right fist high and move the left arm in front of the body, whilst stepping forward with the right foot...

5. ...and down into a right diagonal straddle leg stance, and perform a simultaneous right down block (wrist slightly to the left) and left rising block. *Slow.*

6. Step forward with the left foot whilst crossing the right open hand under the left arm...

Sochin

7. ... land in a left diagonal straddle leg stance and perform a right vertical knife-hand block *Slow* drawing the left fist back to the hip.

8. Perform a left middle area punch...

9. ... and a right middle-area punch in a double action *Fast*.

13. ... land in a right diagonal straddle-leg stance and perform a simultaneous right downward block and left rising block. *Fast*.

Side View

14. Step forward with the left foot whilst crossing the right open hand under the left arm...

Sochin

10. Step with the left foot 90° to the left and cross left arm over the right arm...

11. ...land in a right back stance and perform a double block-left downward block and right inside block to head level. *Fast.*

12. Step forward with the right foot and cross the right arm high, the left arm to the front of the body...

15. ...land in a left diagonal straddle-leg stance and perform a right vertical knife-hand block. *Slow.*

16. Perform a left middle-area punch...

17. ...and a right middle-area punch in a double action. *Fast.*

Sochin

18. Step back with the left foot back and turn 180°, whilst crossing left arm over the right arm...

Front View

19. ...land in a right back stance and perform a double block-left downward block and right inside block to head level. *Fast.*

22. Step forward with the left foot crossing the right open hand under the left arm...

23. ...land in a left diagonal straddle-leg stance and perform a right vertical knife-hand block. *Slow.*

24. Perform a left middle-area punch.

Sochin

Front View

20. Step forward with the right foot with the right arm high, and the left arm in front of the body . . .

21. . . . land in a right diagonal straddle-leg stance and perform a simultaneous right downward block and left rising block. *Fast.*

25. . . . and a right middle-area punch in a double action. *Fast.*

26. Turn 180° to the left and pull the left foot up to the right knee whilst placing the left vertical fist on top of the right fist on the right hip . . .

27. . . . perform a simultaneous left side snap kick and left back fist snap punch. *Fast.*

Sochin

28. As the foot snaps back, step forward...

29. ... into a left diagonal straddle-leg stance and perform a right elbow strike into the left open palm. *Fast*.

30. Look 180° to the right and pull the right foot up to the left knee, whilst placing the right vertical fist on top of the left fist...

34. Turn 180° around to the right and pull the right foot back, pivoting on the left foot – cross the right open hand over the left arm...

Front View

35. ... step through into a left back stance and perform a right knife-hand block. *Fast*.

Sochin

31. ... perform a simultaneous right side snap kick and right back fist snap punch. *Fast*.

32. As the foot snaps back, step forward...

33. ... into a right diagonal straddle-leg stance and perform a left elbow strike into the right open palm. *Fast*.

Front View

36. Look 45° to the left and step with the left foot in that direction whilst crossing the left open hand over the right arm...

37. ... move into a right back stance and perform a left knife-hand block. *Fast*.

Sochin

38. Turn 135° to the left and move the left foot forward whilst crossing the arms in the same direction...

39. ... move into a right back stance and perform a left knife-hand block. *Fast*.

40. Look 45° to the right and move the right foot in that direction, crossing the arms.

Front View

44. Move the left foot forward, crossing the arms...

Front View

Sochin

41. ... move into a left back stance and perform right knife-hand block. *Fast.*

42. Look 45° to the right and move the right foot in that direction, crossing the arms...

43. ... move into a left back stance and perform a right knife-hand block.

45. ... land in a right back stance and perform a left knife-hand block. *Fast.*

Front View

46. Slide both feet forward and at the same time perform a simultaneous left arm (palm down) pressing block and right horizontal spear-hand (palm up) to the face level. *Fast.*

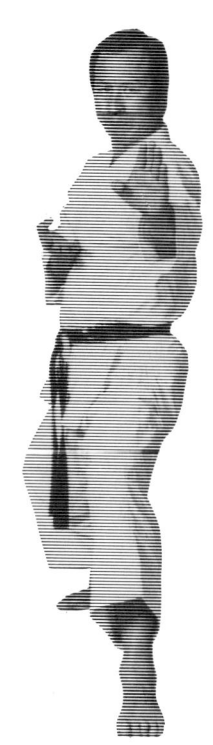

Sochin

Front View

47. Without moving the hand position, perform a left front kick. *Fast*...

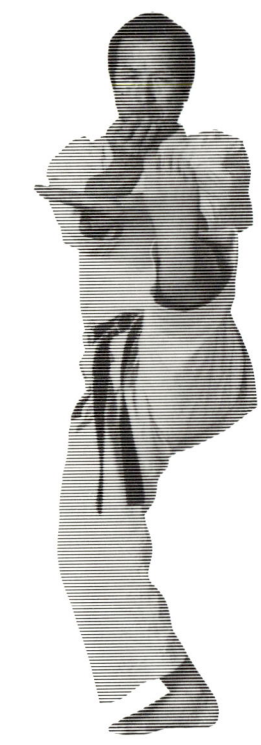

Front View

Front View

50. Perform a right front kick whilst doing a simultaneous block and attack with the arms – a right inner arm twisting block and left close punch, forward, both to head level. *Fast*.

Front View

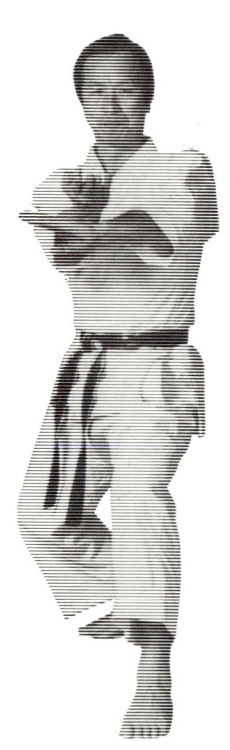

Sochin

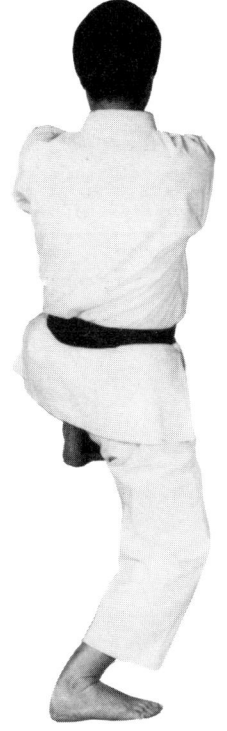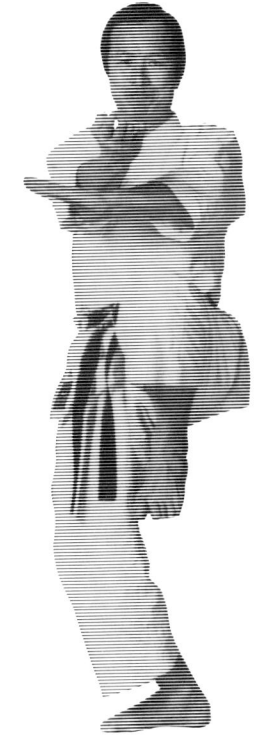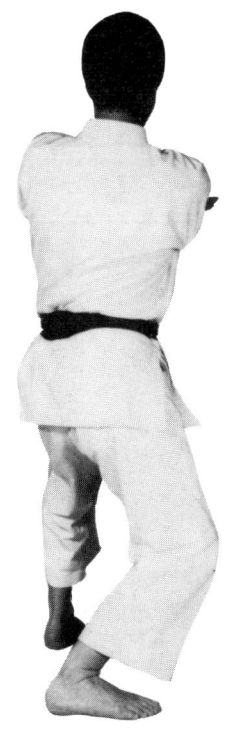

48. ... as the foot snaps back, step forward ...

Front View

49. ... and downward, still keeping hand positions.

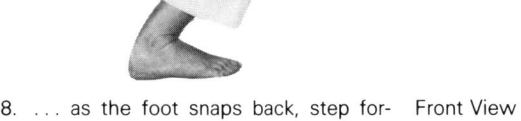

51. As the foot snaps back ...

Front View

52. ... step forward into a right diagonal straddle leg stance and perform a simultaneous left inner arm twisting block and right close punch – by reversing arms. *Fast*.

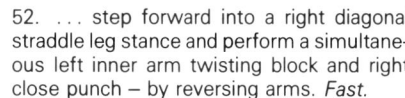

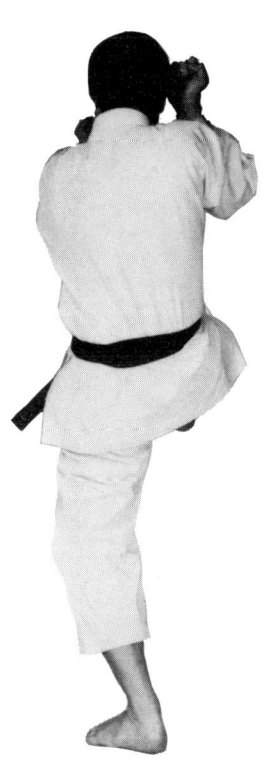

30

Sochin

KIAI

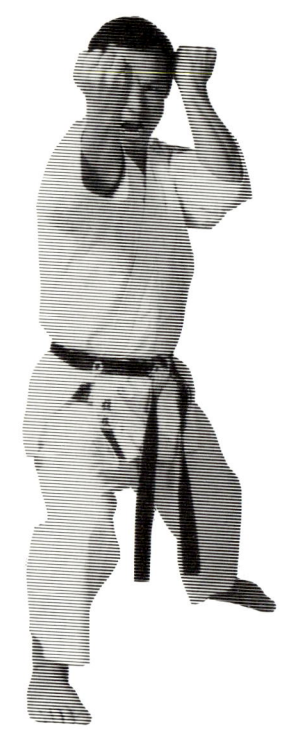

Front View

53. Turn 180° around to the left and straighten the left arm out, palm open . . .

54. . . . swing the right foot (sole) around into the left palm and perform a crescent kick to head level. *Fast.*

58. . . . step into a left diagonal straddle-leg stance and perform a left inside block. *Fast.*

59. Move the right foot forward in the same direction . . .

60. . . . into a right diagonal straddle-leg stance and perform a right stepping punch. *Fast.*

55. Drive your weight forward...

56. ...step into a right diagonal straddle-leg stance and perform a simultaneous right downward block and left rising block. *Fast*.

57. Look 45° to the left, move the left foot in that direction, crossing the left arm under the right arm...

61. Look 90° to the right and move the right foot in that direction crossing the left arm under the right...

62. ...assume a right diagonal straddle-leg stance and perform a right inside block. *Fast*.

63. Move the left foot forward in the same direction...

Sochin

64. ... into a left diagonal straddle-leg stance and perform a left stepping punch. *Fast*.

65. Look 45° to the left (the front) and move the left foot in that direction crossing the left arm under the right ...

66. ... assume a left diagonal straddle-leg stance and perform a left inside block. *Fast*.

70. As the foot snaps back step back ...

71. ... to the previous position pulling the right fist back to chest height and extending the left arm ...

72. ... land in a left diagonal straddle-leg stance and perform a left middle-area punch — the right fist palm down is pulled back to the right side of the chest. *Slow*.

Sochin

67. Without moving the legs cross the right arm into the left...

68. ... and perform a right inside block. *Fast.*

69. Without moving the arms perform a right front kick. *Fast.*

73. Perform a right middle-area punch...

74. ... and a left middle-area punch in a double action. This time the right fist pulls back to the hip. *Fast.*

75. Move the left foot back in line with the right foot, crossing the arms in front of the body...

41

42 **KIAI**

Sochin

Applications

76. ... into the natural stance. (YAME).

1. (5, 13) As your opponent steps in to make his attack, assume a diagonal straddle stance and counter with a left rising block, and right downward block utilising the side of the fist to attack his thigh.

4. (52) Your opponent moves in to attack with a right punch. Adopt a straddle stance, and blocking his punch with a high left inner arm block, retaliate by attacking his throat with a close punch, fist held in a palm up position.

Applications | Sochin

2. Same as Application 1. As the attack is made, adopt a straddle stance and block it with a right down block, performing a left rising block at the same time.

3. (46) As your opponent attacks your body with a right punch, move your feet forward into a small stance, and smother his attack with a pressing block (palm down) while attacking his throat with a right spearhand strike (palm up).

5. (54) From Application 4. As the attack is made to your head from the rear, swing around performing a crescent kick to your opponent's arm to deflect the blow.

6. (72) Intercept your attacker's left punch, drawing it back to your chest and at the same instant, counter-attack with a left punch to his mid-section.

Other Titles published by Dragon Books

Nunchaku Dynamic Training
By Hirokazu Kanazawa 8th Dan

Shadow of the Ninja
By Katsumi Toda

Revenge of the Shogun's Ninja
By Katsumi Toda

Advanced Shotokan Kata Series
By Keinosuke Enoeda 8th Dan

Volume 1
Bassai-Dai : Kanku-Dai : Jion : Empi : Hangetsu

Volume 3
Tekki-Nidan : Tekki-Sandan (2 versions) : Nijushiho : Gojushiho-Dai : Gojushiho-sho (In preparation)

Dynamic Kicking Method
By Masafumi Shiomitsu 7th Dan

The Ninja Star – Art of Shurikenjitsu
By Katsumi Toda

The Kubotan Keychain
By Takayuki Kubota (In preparation)

Sakura Dragon Ltd.
10 Thornbury Road Isleworth Middx TW7 4HG
London England

Sakura Dragon Corporation
P.O. Box 6039 Thousand Oaks California 91359 USA